Animals in Their Habitats

Coral Reef Animals

Francine Galko

Heinemann Library
Chicago, Illinois

Designed by Ginkgo Creative
Printed in China by South China Printing Company

10 09
10 9 8

Library of Congress Cataloging-in-Publication Data
Galko, Francine.
  Coral reef animals / Francine Galko.
     p. cm. -- (Animals in their habitats)
Includes bibliographical references (p.   ).
Summary: Describes coral reefs, the different kinds of animals that can be found in them, and their ecological importance.
  ISBN 1-4034-0177-2 (HC), 1-4034-0434-8 (Pbk.)
  ISBN 978-1-4034-0177-9 (HC), ISBN 978-1-4034-0434-3 (Pbk.)
  1. Coral reef animals--Juvenile literature. [1. Coral reefs and islands. 2. Coral reef animals. 3. Coral reef ecology. 4. Ecology.] I. Title.
  QL125 .G25 2002
  591.77'89--dc21
                            2001007653

Acknowledgments
The author and publishers are grateful to the following for permission to reproduce copyright material:
Cover photograph by Gregory Ochocki/Photo Researchers, Inc.
p. 4 Carl Boes/Bruce Coleman Inc.; p. 5 Douglas Faulkner/Photo Researchers, Inc.; p. 6 Chet Tussey/Gregory Ochocki Productions/Photo Researchers, Inc.; p. 7 Art Wolfe/Photo Researchers, Inc.; p. 8 Joyce and Frank Burek/Animals Animals; pp. 9, 11 Andrew J. Martinez/Photo Researchers, Inc.; pp. 10, 18 Mary Beth Angelo/Photo Researchers, Inc.; p. 12 M. Timothy O'Keefe/Bruce Coleman Inc.; p. 13 James Beveridge/Visuals Unlimited; p. 14 Charles V. Angelo/Photo Researchers, Inc.; p. 15 Ron Seston/Bruce Coleman Inc.; p. 16 David Hall/Photo Researchers, Inc.; p. 17 Chesher/Photo Researchers, Inc.; pp. 19, 20 Zig Leszczynski/Animals Animals; p. 21 Nancy Seston/Photo Researchers, Inc.; p. 22 Carl Roessler/Bruce Coleman Inc.; p. 23 Hal Beral/Visuals Unlimited; p. 24 Marian Bacon/Animals Animals; p. 25 Gregory G. Dimiji/Photo Researchers, Inc.; p. 26 Michele Westermorland; p. 27 P. Harrison/OSF/Animals Animals; p. 28 A. Flowers and L. Newman/Photo Researchers, Inc.; p. 29 Gregory Ochocki/Photo Researchers, Inc.
Every effort has been made to contact copyright holders of any material reproduced in this book. Any omissions will be rectified in subsequent printings if notice is given to the publisher.

Some words are shown in bold, **like this.** You can find out what they mean by looking in the glossary.

To learn more about the coral reef on the cover, turn to page 29.

Contents

What Is a Coral Reef?

A coral reef is a kind of **habitat.** It is a group of plants and animals that live together underwater. A coral reef is made of the skeletons of animals called **coral polyps.** Coral polyps grow on the seafloor.

When a coral polyp dies, more polyps come to live right on top of its body. In this way, the polyps build up a reef like the walls of a house.

Where Are Coral Reefs?

Coral reefs are found only in certain places. They form in shallow water where there is sunlight, warm weather, and clean, salty water.

Coral reefs often grow along rocky **shores.** Coral reefs called **barrier reefs** are just off the shore. **Atolls** are coral reef islands.

Coral Reef Homes

Animals like squids live in the water around a coral reef. The reef squid swims in shallow water looking for food.

Spotted scorpion fishes live on the rocks and coral on the shallow sea bottom. The spines on the back of this fish can sting.

Living in the Lagoon

The water between the reef and the land is the **lagoon.** The water is calm in lagoons. Large snails called queen conchs often live here among the seagrass and fishes.

Different kinds of sea cucumbers also live in lagoons. The donkey dung sea cucumber has **tentacles.** It pulls in its tentacles when it is bothered.

Living on the Crest

Some reefs form a hill out in the **ocean**.
The top of the hill is called the reef **crest**.
Elkhorn **coral polyps** sometimes make up
most of a reef crest.

Green colonial anemones often grow just behind the reef crest. They eat pieces of elkhorn coral that have been broken off by strong waves.

Living on the Reef Front

The **reef front** faces the sea. Like most reef animals, the **iridescent** tube **sponge** lives on the reef front. This sponge can glow during the daytime.

A parrotfish has hundreds of teeth.
It uses its teeth to scrape off pieces
of coral.

Living Inside Other Animals

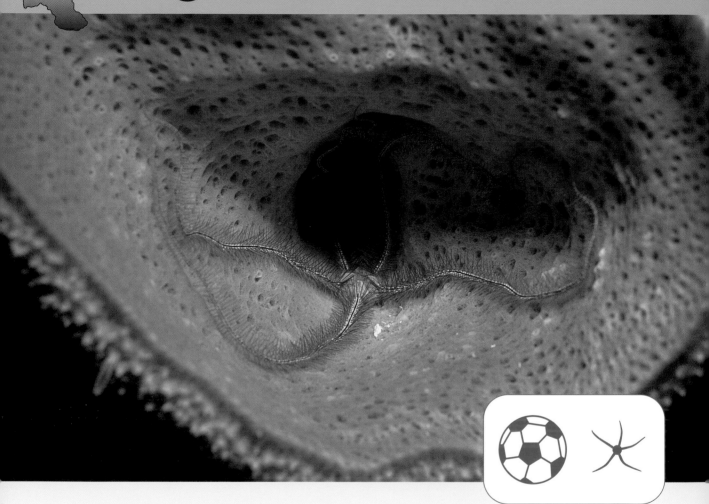

Some coral reef animals live inside other animals. Brittle stars often live inside **sponges**. A sponge looks like a plant, but it's an animal.

Pearlfishes live inside some sea cucumbers.
They come out at night to eat. Then,
they wiggle back inside the cucumber,
past its teeth.

Living Among Tentacles

Cleaner shrimp live among the **tentacles** of giant Caribbean anemones. They clean the anemone's tentacles by eating tiny animals that grow on them.

Anemones live on the shells of star-eyed hermit crabs. They scare off the crab's **predators** and eat food left over from the crab's meals.

Finding Food in a Coral Reef

Porcupine fishes eat a lot of reef animals that live in shells. They use their strong jaws and teeth to crush the shells.

The pipes-of-pan **sponge** pulls water in through holes in its sides. It eats tiny plants and animals in the water. Then, it spits out the water through a big hole on top.

Coral Reef Predators

Predators hunt other animals in the reef. Moray eels are reef predators. They hide most of the time. At night, they look for sleeping fishes to eat.

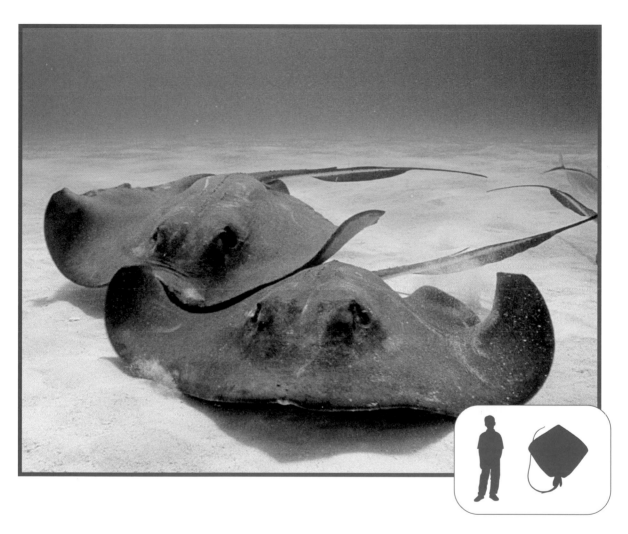

Stingrays catch clams, crabs, and other animals that live in the sand on the **ocean** floor. A stingray uses its fins to put **prey** in its mouth.

Hiding in a Coral Reef

Many animals in the coral reef are hard
to see because they have **camouflage**.
This grouper fish blends into the reef.
Can you see it?

The trumpetfish hides by acting like
a branch of **coral polyp**. It stretches
out and moves the same way the coral
branches do.

Coral Reef Babies

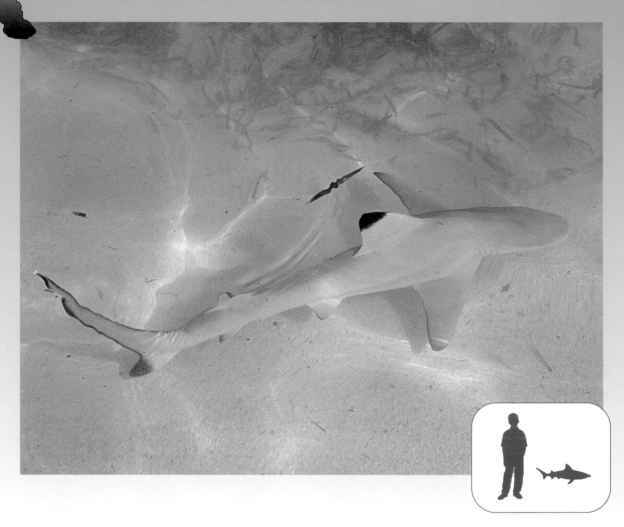

There are many kinds of baby animals on a coral reef. Young blacktip reef sharks have black tips on their back and side fins, like adults. They first eat on their own in the shallow reef waters.

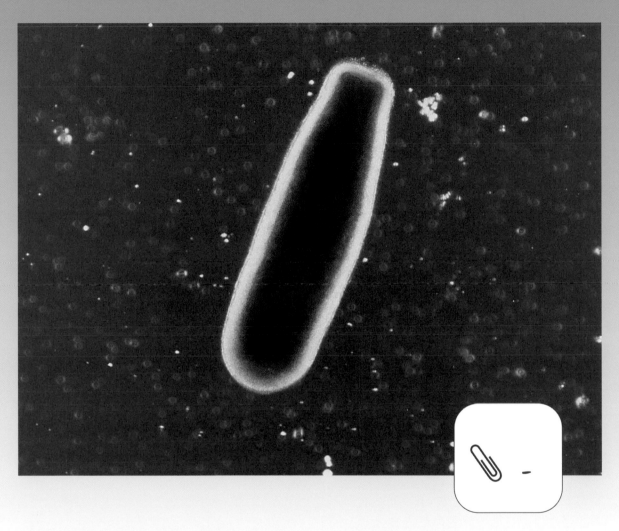

Coral polyps, like the common rose coral, make babies called **larvae.** The larvae swim to the **ocean** floor. Each larva grows into an adult coral polyp.

Protecting Coral Reef Animals

Sometimes people take fishes and other animals from coral reefs. They sell them in pet stores. Touching or stepping on **coral polyps** can hurt a coral reef.

Do not buy coral reef animals or their shells. If you swim near a coral reef, do not touch it. Let's keep coral reefs clean and safe for the animals that live there.

 # Glossary

atoll coral reef island

barrier reef coral reef that is in the water, just away from land

camouflage way an animal hides itself

coral polyp body of a sea animal that is attached to something

crest tallest part of a coral reef

habitat place where an animal lives

iridescent showing a rainbow of colors, like a soap bubble does in the light

lagoon water between the land and a coral reef

larva (more than one are called larvae) young form of some animals

ocean all the saltwater that covers Earth

predator animal that hunts and eats other animals

prey animal that is hunted and eaten by another animal

reef front shallow part of a reef that faces the ocean

shore land next to the sea or other water

sponge animal that lives in the ocean; looks like a kitchen sponge

tentacle long, finger-shaped part of an animal's body that often catches food or stings prey

More Books to Read

Bearanger, Marie and Eric Ethan. *Coral Reef Feeders.*
Milwaukee: Gareth Stevens, Inc., 1997.

Llewellyn, Claire. *Coral Reefs.* Chicago: Heinemann Library,
2000.

Stone, Lynn M. *Animals of the Coral Reef.* Vero Beach, Fla.:
Rourke Publishing, LLC, 2001.

Index